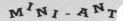
D0823515

media MIX

Sharon Siamon

James Barry

Published in 1994 simultaneously by:

Nelson Canada, *and* The Wright Group
A Division of Thomson 19201 – 120th Avenue NE
   Canada Limited Bothell, Washington
1120 Birchmount Road 98011-9512
Scarborough, Ontario U.S.A.
M1K 5G4
Canada

ISBN 0-17-604365-9 ISBN 0-17-604398-5

1 2 3 4 5 /WC/ 97 96 95 94 93 1 2 3 4 5 /WC/ 97 96 95 94 93

I(T)P™
International Thomson Publishing
The trademark ITP is used under license

As requested by individual copyright holders, some selections
may retain original spellings, punctuation, usage, and style of
measurement.

Project Manager/Development: Lana Kong
Assistant Editor: Carolyn Madonia
Senior Production Editor: Deborah Lonergan
Art Direction: Bruce Bond
Cover Design: Liz Nyman
Cover Illustration: Avner Levona

Printed and bound in Canada

Canadian Cataloguing in Publication Data

Main entry under title:
Media mix

(Nelson mini-anthologies)
ISBN 0-17-604365-9

1. Readers (Secondary). 2. Readers – Mass media.
3. Mass media – Literary collections. I. Siamon,
Sharon. II. Barry, James, 1939–   . III. Series.

PE1121.M44   1994   428.6   C93-095399-1

Series Review Panel

Table of Contents

MOVIE MAGIC

MEET THE PRESS: Newspapers and Magazines

ON THE AIR: Television and Radio

Photographs follow page 48.

Movie Magic

▲▽▷▽▷▲▽▷▽▽▲▽▷▽▷▲▽▷▷▷

MOTHER GOOSE AND GRIMM
by Mike Peters

▲▽▷▽▷▲▽▷▽▽▲▽▷▽▷▲▽▷▷▷

▲ ▼ ▶ ▼ ▶ ▲ ▼ ▶ ▼ ▶ ▲ ▼ ▶ ▼ ▶ ▲ ▼ ▶ ▼ ▶ ▶

MOVIE TRIVIA

Collected by Todd Mercer

Most extras ever used in a movie (*Gandhi*, 1982):
300 000

Character who appears most frequently in horror
films: Count Dracula (162). His nearest competi-
tor: Frankenstein's monster (112)

Number of cars wrecked in the most destructive car
chase ever filmed (*The Junkman*): 150

Seating capacity for the largest cinema ever built,
the New York Roxy: 6214

Cost of creating 50 computer-generated shots, occu-
pying a total of five minutes of screen time in
Terminator 2: $7.55 million

Most movies seen by a single person, 1953–1991:
20 064

The average number of letters used in a movie
title: 17

Most letters used in a single word in a film title: 52
in *Schwarzhuhnbraunhuhnschwarzhyhnweisshuhn-
rothuhnweiss oder Put-Putt*, a West German film

Number of hours spent on the sea bottom filming the IMAX movie *Titanica*: 140

Percentage of 1000 adults polled who said they would pay extra in movie theatres to order and receive refreshments at their seats: 30%

And those who would pay extra for seats assigned according to height: 50%

SPECIAL-EFFECTS DINOSAURS LOOK LIKE THE REAL THING

by Craig MacInnis

Those special-effects wizards combined computer imagery and models to create the incredibly life-like dinosaurs of the movie *Jurassic Park*.

Even before its 1993 release in theatres across North America, *Jurassic Park* had been widely called a landmark film for its innovations in dinosaur technology. The Industrial Light And Magic special-effects outfit has been able to use computer graphics to create completely digital animation[1] of animals.

The effect is stunning.

Most critics who saw *Jurassic Park* felt there was little difference between ILM's computer imagery and live-action photography.

ILM's Dennis Muren, a winner of seven

Academy Awards for his work on films such as *Terminator 2, E.T.*, and *Return Of The Jedi*, was in charge of creating the full-motion dinosaurs.

"We didn't know at the start of production if we could get computer images to look photo-real," Muren told me in L.A. "We had two big problems. One is, are they going to look photo-real so you don't think it's a computer or it's plastic or anything like that. And then it had to *move*. The performance you can get now with computer-generated images is just phenomenal."

Muren says several extended shots—particularly of the film's brachiosaurus and T-rex—not only produced life-like physical motion "but (from watching them) you can begin to understand the character of the animals and what they're thinking."

This last claim may be going a bit far, but there's no question that *Jurassic Park* brings its four-legged inhabitants to life well enough to satisfy most late-20th century consumers, if not fossil experts. In fact, the film's technical staff relied heavily on the advice of Jack Horner, a Montana-based researcher considered the leading dinosaur authority in the world.

Jurassic Park's other major breakthrough comes from the Stan Winston Studio, which used more than 60 artists, engineers, and puppeteers to create life-size versions of a 4000-kg, 12-m-long T-rex, a 2-m velociraptor, a long-necked brachiosaurus, and the "sick" triceratops seen lying on its side in a scene with Laura Dern's scientist character.

"Dinosaur movies have been made before and they've been made beautifully," says Winston, the special-effects wizard who drew inspiration from the classics while hoping to improve upon them.

"*King Kong* (1933) is a wonderful dinosaur movie, so, if *King Kong* is already there, we knew there was no reason why we couldn't do *Jurassic Park*," says Winston. "We knew there would be technologies that we could fall back on (old "go-motion" puppets) if we couldn't in fact do what we were setting out to do.

"But we were able to do everything that we set out to do. It was beyond anything we felt we could accomplish."

In all, Winston's studio crafted nine different dinosaur species, including the venom-spewing dilophosaurs, the vicious velociraptors, and a cute little hatchling. Constructed from a variety of materials, including latex, foam rubber, and urethane, the level of detail used for the animated dinosaurs included flaring nostrils and saliva-covered teeth.

1. **digital animation:** a process in which the computer draws the pictures instead of an artist drawing them by hand

▲▼▶▼▶▲▼▶▼▼▲▼▶▼▼▲▼▶▼▲▶

THE GOLDEN AGE
OF LAUGHTER

by Max Braithwaite

Max Braithwaite, who is in his 80s, still laughs at a funny movie as hard as he did when he was a boy watching silent movies in Prince Albert, Saskatchewan.

The best thing about Prince Albert was the Strand Theatre on Central Avenue. It was a temple of delight, an arena of excitement, a steam bath of emotions, a great place to be on Saturday afternoon. Movies on Saturday afternoon cost a nickel for kids, and on Friday night they cost a dime. So, of course, we always wanted to go on Friday night. But there weren't enough dimes to go around.

We'd line up at Dad's chair after lunch on Saturday and he would dig deep into his pocket with his big hand and produce a handful of change. Then, with a long finger, he'd poke among the dimes and quarters and coppers, looking for nickels. (I remember that there was always a shiny lucky quarter in that big, lean hand. Dad had carried it in his pocket since he was a schoolteacher in Ontario.) Then he'd dole out the nickels, and we'd be off.

For a long time Denny, my younger brother, got in free, so my other brother Hub and I would take him with us. Dad, who paid little attention to these niceties, didn't know about the free ticket and so he gave us a nickel for Denny, too. Which meant a whole raft of cent candy, licorice plugs, licorice whips, jaw-breakers, and candy kisses to be munched during the performance.

We worked this racket until long after Denny was six. He was a skinny kid and small and the ticket-seller got used to letting him in free. But they changed ticket-sellers, and when we appeared the new one asked,

"How old is the little red-headed boy?"

"Oh, he's just five," Hub assured her.

But he hadn't reckoned on Denny's pride of accomplishment in having achieved his sixth birthday three months earlier. He elbowed his way to the front with fire shooting from his eyes and stated defiantly, "I'm not five. I'm six!" That was the end of our nickel's worth of goodies during the show.

Inside that dark theatre it was bedlam. Every kid that came considered it his duty to make as much noise and create as much mayhem as possible. We always arrived at least a half-hour before the show started, and for some silly reason they let us in (the practice of making kids line up outside on the sidewalk evidently hadn't been considered). So, we whiled away the time wrestling, stealing each other's toques and mitts, shoving each other under the seats, chasing each other up and down the aisles, and yelling our heads off.

Then—at last—would come the long-awaited signal. The lights would go out, and the trademark of the Union Operator would flash on the screen. And the roar was such as greets a tie-breaking home run in the ninth with two out. And when the movie began there was still no need to be quiet. There was no talk or sound—except what came from the eager piano player in the pit—and all the dialogue was printed on the screen. So you could cheer with the good guy, scream at the bad guy, and laugh your head off at the funny guy without ever interrupting the action.

And what action! It was all action then. We'd see at least four items. A feature, usually starring William S. Hart, or Doug Fairbanks, or Hoot Gibson, or Milton Sills, or Thomas Meighen. They were the greatest: plenty of fist-fights, thousands of blank cartridges blazed away, breakneck chases, crashing aircraft, exploding ships. Talk about violence! They were loaded with violence.

And then came the serial. Continued from last week, when the heroine, always in riding breeches, had been bound hand and foot and locked inside a shack which was perched precariously on the edge of a cliff. The villain, bad luck to him, had planted a charge of dynamite—they used more dynamite in the movies than they did in construction in those days—and was lurking behind a boulder, ready to push the plunger down and blow shack and heroine to eternity.

But it never worked out that way. The hero, you see, was on the way. He always got there in the nick of time and saved her life. Then she would throw her arms around his neck, and kiss him, and flutter her eyelashes, and such a "boo!" went up from the disgusted boys in the audience as could be heard clear down River Street.

And then there was the comedy, which we all loved. One- and two-reelers, featuring Charlie Chaplin, or Fatty Arbuckle, or cross-eyed Chester Conklin, or wistful Harry Langdon, or deadpan Buster Keaton. There was always a chase with automobiles just missing each other on busy streets, with men piling out of them and flying through windows, and lots of prat-falls—the pie in the face came much later—and the Keystone Cops, and the Mack Sennett bathing beauties.

It was all pantomime[1], and it killed us. I have never heard such laughter as arose from those Saturday afternoon audiences. Never since have I laughed so hard that I couldn't get my breath, that my stomach pained, that I literally fell out into the aisle. Yes, I admit it, more than once our bladders couldn't stand the strain, and many a wet-legged kid staggered embarrassed out of the Strand. No generation of kids ever laughed as hard as we did, I'm sure, and none had so much to laugh at. It was truly the golden age of laughter.

1. pantomime: a type of acting where no sound is used, but actors express feelings by body and facial movement

▲ ▼ ▶ ▼ ▶ ▲ ▼ ▶ ▼ ▶ ▲ ▼ ▶ ▼ ▶ ▲ ▼ ▶ ▼ ▶ ▶

CHARLIE CHAPLIN, THE LITTLE TRAMP

by Lorraine Monk

He was the first big Hollywood star, way back when movies were new. And, without speaking a word, he made people all over the world laugh, and cry.

Even from behind, Charlie Chaplin may have been the most recognized figure in the world. Recognized, that is, not as himself, but as the Little Tramp. It was a character he created for himself in 1914 and which today still has the power to evoke laughter and tears from adoring fans on every continent of the globe. Charlie Chaplin mastered the art of pantomime and slapstick as no other actor has ever done. Sporting an ill-fitting frock coat, baggy pants, bowler hat, and oversized shoes, he strutted across the screen carrying a bamboo cane that seemed to have a mischievous mind of its own.

Chaplin became the first Hollywood star to win an international reputation; his characters became the stuff of folklore and legends. In his lifetime, Chaplin made some 225 films. Most of them, incredibly, he wrote and directed himself.

Chaplin's photograph, depicting the tender-hearted Little Tramp, is perhaps the most famous motion picture "still" in the history of the movies. He symbolized the little person's struggle against the system, and he won hearts all over the world with his portrayal of one person's (often amusing) attempts to change the way things are. With his antics and his comic genius, he succeeded in turning a rather sad old world, briefly, into a very funny place. And for that great gift of laughter he has been called the greatest theatrical artist of all time.

▲ ▼ ▶ ▼ ▶ ▲ ▼ ▶ ▼ ▶ ▲ ▼ ▶ ▼ ▶ ▲ ▼ ▶ ▼ ▶ ▶

THREE-KLEENEX MOVIES

by Peg Kehret

Some people think crying over a movie is silly, but others enjoy a good weepy picture.

There are many kinds of movies—horror movies, comedies, adventure films, romances. But the kind of movie I like best doesn't have any particular category. I like a movie that makes me cry.

There are degrees of sadness in these movies. Some only make me misty-eyed. In a Misty Movie, I can blink several times and the moisture evaporates or I can pretend to scratch my ear while I wipe away any trace of tears. That way, the person I'm with doesn't suspect that I'm misty-eyed. Misty Movies are usually good but not the kind you want to see more than once or urge all your friends to see.

One step up on the sad-movie success ladder are the Tricklers. In a Trickler Movie, I go just a bit further. The tears will well up and then gradually overflow from one eye and trickle down my cheek. It isn't a steady stream of tears, merely a single trickle, and I can adjust my glasses or brush my hair back or use some other excuse to bring my hand to my face and get rid of the tear before anyone notices it.

When I attend a Trickler Movie with my friends, we watch each other out of the corners of our eyes. Everyone wants to see if the other people are crying or not. Probably the Trickler Movies would affect me even more if I wasn't watching my friends and knowing they are watching me.

Despite our attempts to appear unmoved in a Trickler Movie, we all agree that the very best movies of all are the Three-Kleenex Movies, where all control of our tears is abandoned. In a Three-Kleenex Movie, you have no choice but to wipe your eyes—several times—and blow your nose and let the whole world know you're crying. These are the movies where I watch all the credits at the end, not because I care who did the make-up or ran the camera, but because I need those extra minutes to compose myself so I'm not sobbing as I leave the theatre.

Many of the classic animal films, like *Dumbo* and *Bambi*, are Three-Kleenex Movies, but I've been known to weep and blow over people stories, too.

Three-Kleenex Movies are best seen in a theatre. If you watch them on television or a VCR at home, it just isn't the same. For one thing, there is usually a light on and that inhibits your reactions somewhat. Also, because the screen is smaller, the characters don't seem quite as real.

A theatre is an impersonal place, a place where I can cry anonymously. I can lose myself in the story and weep for the people on the screen. It's a form of catharsis[1] because I always feel better afterwards.

Tears are good for the movie business. Any time I see a movie that makes me cry, I'm sure to tell all my friends to go to it. They do the same for me.

Perhaps Hollywood needs a new rating system. Forget the PG and the R categories. If they really want people to line up at the ticket window, rate the movie Three-Kleenex. I guarantee it'll be a success.

1. **catharsis:** emotional release

THE PEOPLE IN MOVIES

No, we're not talking about movie stars. Here's a glossary of people who work behind the scenes to bring a motion picture together.

The **producer** raises the money to make the movie and sees to it that everything runs smoothly.

The **director** is in charge of making the movie: "I get the right actors, the right music, the right costumes, and the right sets … I hope."

The **casting director** helps choose the actors.

The **production designer** is responsible for the sets and everything else in front of the camera.

The **special-effects crew** builds miniatures and makes them look like huge landscapes, or creates computer images to be combined with film of the actors.

The **cinematographer** creates the photographic look of the picture, its visual style and colour.

The **music director** helps choose a composer to write the score.

The **sound department** makes sure the dialogue, music, and other sound effects are mixed together right.

The **editor** takes the many different pieces of film, shot at different angles, and puts them together to create the final movie.

The **publicist** tells magazines, newspapers, and TV stations about the movie studio's films.

▲ ▶ ▼ ▶ ▲ ▼ ▶ ▼ ▲ ▶ ▼ ▶ ▲ ▼ ▶ ▼ ▶

BEHIND THE SCENES: CASTING AGENT AND SET BUILDER

from *TG Magazine*

Thinking of a career in film? Meet Laela Weinzweig and David Melrose, two people who are following their dream of working in movies.

Casting Agent

In the morning the breakdowns come in from directors outlining all their projects. Casting agent Laela Weinzweig will know what's shooting in town, where, and what kind of actors are needed. She examines the breakdown and pulls pictures and résumés from her files, then types a lengthy note to the casting directors for each performer, giving reasons why her actor is perfect for the role.

"Then I hound them, and sell.... A talent

agent is like a mother," Laela laughs.

She works with actors to prepare them for an audition. "I try to get the 'sides' (a copy of the part of the actual script which will be shot) ahead of time and I will call my clients and go over the part with them…. That's how I use my casting experi-ence. I know what the director is looking for; I want my actors to go into the session totally prepared."

The luxury of being a casting director or an agent is that you can leave the office and work from home. Laela has an at-home survival kit: a binder with all the casting directors' names and fax numbers, and information on all her clients, with pictures, résumés, and other important informa-tion. Anyone can call her when they're missing information or want to contact one of her clients.

The atmosphere in a casting agent's office is the same informal one you will find in the film industry as a whole. No one dresses up to go to work, and you're solely responsible for getting the job done. If you wish to start at 10 a.m. or leave at 2 p.m., it's up to you. A casting agent works for salary plus commission[1], so the responsibility is on you to increase your earnings. Working with a commission, there is always the potential of greater income in the future from today's success.

It's a competitive career, with no formal education. It comes from understanding the film industry … you begin at the bottom and learn.

Laela recommends that you begin in a casting office as a receptionist, "gofer," or assistant, and pay attention. Learn everybody's job; don't take for granted what everyone is doing. As a talent agent you will have to know how to sell someone and how to negotiate, which includes understanding the union rules. To be a good casting agent, you have to understand the film and TV industry, be outgoing and a quick thinker.

"We're all in it because we enjoy it; I could never do any other kind of job!" The casting agents are agents for actors. Directors work with the producer to find the right acting talent for a series, film, or documentary. These two people, the agent and the director, are the fuel which keeps actors on screens in Canadian films.

While the agent's job is to sell the talent of the people he or she represents, a director's job is to give a brief summary of the story with a brief character description, and inform agents about the types of actors needed. Laela has worked on both sides since starting her own casting company.

Set Builder

Imagine! A forced-perspective room, only 1.5 m high at one end and almost 5 m at the other. The door is built out of rubber, so it will look like the room is breathing.

Not your normal carpenter's job, but it's life for David Melrose.

As an assistant carpenter, David has worked on TV series such as *Captain Power*, *The Twilight Zone*, *My Secret Identity*, *War of the Worlds*, and *Friday's Curse*.

Film carpentry is interesting work. It's a lot of fun because you never know what will come next. You work on interesting sets, building things you'd never come across in regular construction. There are many fascinating projects in film which require creativity to accomplish.

"Being a carpenter in film is the cream of the construction field. In the 'real world' you have to specialize as a framer or cabinet-maker, but in film you get to do it all," says Melrose.

When *Captain Power* began production, David was hired to move the production office and set up the studio in a large, old public-transit warehouse. He built the wardrobe, hair and make-up rooms, and the administration offices. When he was done, the construction manager for the production offered him a job as a construction labourer.

As a labourer on the set, David learned a lot about carpentry and about working in the construction department.

Compared to other departments in film production, the construction department is very structured. They will work a nine-hour day with two 15-minute breaks and a half-hour for lunch. After nine hours the carpenters are entitled to overtime pay.

Most carpenters in the construction department will work their way up from being labourers. To become a labourer, only basic carpentry skills are needed. The ability to read blueprints, which can be learned in a basic drafting course, is a definite asset, as are high-school math courses. It is very important to have at least grade 12 math skills, as there is a lot of work to do with angles, which translates into plenty of geometry.

Freelance film carpenters come from a variety of backgrounds: some specialize in cabinet-making when unemployed in film, while others have a background in residential construction. Each individual's specialty makes him or her valuable to the production.

The construction manager receives blueprints from the art director and estimates the cost of building a particular set. He's responsible for the budget in the construction department and will pass the drawings (once they're approved) on to his head carpenter. The head carpenter will distribute the work according to skill.

David describes his job as "working on a giant puzzle. Everyone is building one piece of it, and it must fit."

1. commission: a fee paid to a salesperson or agent for every sale he or she makes

▲▼►▼▲▼►▼▲▲▼►▼▲▼►▼▲▼►▼►►

INTO THE FUTURE WITH MOVIES

by Deborah Hitzeroth and Sharon Heerboth

One day soon we will not simply watch movies, but participate in them as well.

In the future, people will no longer simply watch films but will experience them. Instead of being windows to other worlds, movies will be doors to walk through. In the future, audiences will no longer be passive viewers but active participants in films.

Ride a Magic Carpet

The move from simply watching a film to experiencing it started in 1990 when IMAX Systems Corporation began testing the Magic Carpet System. When the system is perfected, perhaps within the next five years, it will allow audiences to feel as if they are riding a magic carpet through a movie instead of viewing it on a screen.

To enhance the reality of a film, viewers will be totally surrounded by images. In the Magic Carpet System, the main viewing screen will be seven stories tall. In addition, there will be screens on the sides, ceiling, and floor of the theatre. These screens will help immerse the audience in the movie. If a film includes a flight scene, for example, clouds will be projected above, below, and around the audience. Surrounded by these visions, viewers should experience the feeling of floating through the sky. In an ocean sequence, audiences will be able to experience the feeling of living underwater. Sharks will swim by viewers, and schools of fish will dart above them.

Touching New Worlds

While scientists work to perfect the Magic Carpet System, other researchers are working to take audiences one step farther. When perfected, computer-generated virtual reality will create new worlds that audiences can reach out and touch. A number of U.S. and other foreign companies are working on the concept.

To enter virtual reality, the participant wears specially designed gloves and goggles linked to a sophisticated computer. The goggles contain two video screens, one for each eye. The screens show three-dimensional scenes that seem to totally surround the wearer. Instead of sitting passively, viewers leave their chairs and walk through movie scenes. Every time a viewer moves his or her head or hands, electronic sensors inside the goggles and gloves send signals to the computer. The computer then changes the images on the video screens to match the viewer's new position.

If a film contained a shot of a house, for example, the viewer could actually take a walking tour of the entire house. Following the movements of the goggles and gloves, the computer would be able to present an accurate image of the house. With the help of the sensors and computer, the viewer could walk down corridors, peer around corners, or glance over a shoulder to see if anyone is following.

The wearer would experience the feeling of touching and picking up things in the film. Using the special gloves, viewers could open doors or pick up books from a shelf. A pressing sensation supplied by the gloves would give the wearer a real sense of feeling something, even though the wearer would be touching nothing.

Is It Live or Just a Computer Image?

... In the past, movies were made with images captured on film. In the future, computers may eliminate the need for film altogether....

Bob Schneider, a professor of video and film at Southwestern College in Chula Vista, California, says, "As we move into computers, which generate images on their own, we may move away from photographs. It would even be possible to create a feature film that is populated with human characters that are not human but are all completely computer-generated. If you create computer characters, you can have them do things that humans can't do."...

Computer characters could easily fly, or change shape, or do whatever a director required, stunts that now can be performed only with the help of expensive special effects....

As the computer film systems are perfected, moviegoers may be able to custom-design the movies they watch. Such films, called interactive films, would allow viewers to choose actions for the screen heroes. For example, in a science-fiction thriller, a viewer could decide if the hero fights an alien or flees simply by pushing a button. The viewer's choice would determine the next scene in the film. This interactive feature would give a single film hundreds of possible story lines.

Interactive films may also be linked with virtual reality to make the computer-generated worlds more realistic. Researchers at Carnegie-Mellon University in Pittsburgh, Pennsylvania, are already working on combining the two technologies. Researchers hope to make computer-generated characters who can adapt to the actions of the audience....

As new technology replaces old filmmaking techniques, the movies will take us to places that we can now reach only in our imagination.

2

Meet the Press:
Newspapers and Magazines

▲▽▼▶▲▼▶▽▼▲▼▶▼▲▼▶▼▶▶

SHOE
by Jeff MacNelly

▲▽▼▶▲▼▶▽▼▲▼▶▼▲▼▶▼▶▶

▲ ▶ ▼ ▶ ▲ ▼ ▶ ▼ ▶ ▲ ▼ ▶ ▼ ▶ ▲ ▼ ▶ ▼ ▶ ▶

NEWSPAPER AND MAGAZINE TRIVIA

Collected by Todd Mercer

Newspaper Trivia

Daily circulation of Canada's largest newspaper, *The Toronto Star*: 511 696

Highest circulation of any newspaper in the world, *Komsomolskaya Pravda*, the youth paper of the former Soviet Communist Party: 21 975 000

Number of trees it takes to make the newsprint for the Sunday edition of *The New York Times*: 63 000

Quantity of waste newspaper thrown out by the average household in a year: 150 kg

Estimated readership of the most syndicated columnist, *Ann Landers*: 96 000 000

Number of clues in the largest crossword puzzle ever published: 12 489 across and 13 125 down

Number of newspapers bought daily per 1000 people in Japan: 575

Number of newspapers bought daily per 1000 people in Iceland: 420

Most misprints on a newspaper page: 97

Number of newspapers in which *Peanuts*, the most syndicated cartoon strip, appears: 2300

Magazine Trivia

Weight of the heaviest magazine ever published, American *Vogue* (808 pages): 1.51 kg

Number of pages in the bulkiest consumer magazine ever published, *Hong Kong Toys*: 1356

Total U.S. spending for magazine advertising: $6 515 200 000

Cost of buying the complete monthly lineup of Marvel comic books for four months: $510

Number of *Archie*, *Veronica*, and *Jughead* comic books purchased by Canadians on an average day: 14 521

Number of copies of *The National Enquirer* purchased by Canadians on an average day: 114 286

Circulation of *People* magazine: 3 380 832

Circulation of *Teen* magazine: 1 161 734

▲▼▶▲▼▲▼▶▲▼▶▼▲▼▶▼▲▶

ANNIE LEIBOVITZ
SHOOTS TO SUCCESS

by Becky Siamon

How would you like to photograph The
Rolling Stones backstage after a big concert?
Or shoot portraits of famous movie stars in
their own homes? Photographer Annie
Leibovitz has the stars coming to her to have
their pictures taken.

Annie Leibovitz, the photographer, has become
Annie Leibovitz, the celebrity. Her rise to super-
stardom reads like a young person's dream come
true.

In 1970, Annie showed up at the office of
Rolling Stone magazine in San Francisco, carrying
her portfolio of photographs. At the age of 20, she
had just returned from a year on a kibbutz in Israel.
Her only contact with the art world had been as a
student at the San Francisco Art Institute. She was

shy, almost 180 cm tall, and totally unknown.

Once inside the *Rolling Stone* office, however, Annie managed to get her portfolio viewed by the art director, Robert Kingsbury. He was so impressed with her work that he hired her for a shoot in New York City. The assignment? To photograph John Lennon of the Beatles. The following month, Annie's portrait of John Lennon was on the cover of *Rolling Stone*.

Over the next ten years, Annie's work with *Rolling Stone* would establish her as the most famous magazine photographer in North America. She became known for her original and eye-catching portraits of celebrities—and the stars loved her. She made them look good.

Some of her most famous portraits—of The Rolling Stones, Woody Allen, Bette Midler, Steve Martin, Robert Redford, Bruce Springsteen, and Meryl Streep—have appeared in magazines around the globe. More recently, as a photographer for *Vanity Fair*, Annie has generated controversy with her photos of actress Demi Moore.

When taking a portrait, Annie sometimes likes to move in temporarily with her subject. This way she can photograph them when they have lots of time and are more open to the lens. Annie says, "When I say I want to photograph someone, what I really mean is I like to get to know them."

Often, Annie's pictures are as much the subject's inspiration as her own. Her portrait of Meryl Streep was inspired by the fact that the actress was sick and tired of being photographed as a "famous actress." Meryl felt she was nobody special, just a working actress. So Annie suggested Meryl paint her face like a mime. Meryl then came up with the idea of pulling her face like a rubber mask, creating an unforgettable image.

Annie enjoys shaking up people's expectations, sometimes going against a person's usual image. For her portrait of Lauren Hutton, Annie decided to photograph the usually glamorous model covered in mud and grass, except for her face. Annie wanted to show, in a witty way, that Lauren was not only beautiful, but down to earth.

Wit and humour, in fact, are Annie's trademarks. Her portrait of comedian Rodney Dangerfield shows him looking frazzled and helpless while holding a discouraged, diapered baby. Then there's Clint Eastwood standing in a dusty western setting—tightly tied up.

Annie likes to present a great deal of information in a single powerful image, rather than use a group of photos. This is partly a result of her stint at *Rolling Stone*, since a cover photo has to "sell" the magazine. And she finds that letting people be themselves makes more of a statement than if they are doing something really out of character.

Annie takes her work very seriously, but tries to balance her life so that she isn't taking pictures all the time. It's important, she believes, to have a separate life from which to draw experiences and ideas. Otherwise, she says, you start to cheat yourself and your pictures.

No longer shy, Annie Leibovitz has herself become a celebrity as the foremost photographer of famous and talented people. Whenever she makes a bookstore appearance to promote one of her photography books, she finds people lined up for hours to get her autograph. But, more than a media photographer and a star, she's an artist with a camera.

UNFORGETTABLE PHOTOS

"A picture is worth a thousand words."

Have you ever seen a picture that stops you dead in your tracks? Maybe it is a ballplayer, leaping to make a game-winning catch. Maybe it's the face of a starving child. Perhaps a famous rock star. Whatever the image, you know you won't forget it for a long time.

The first six pictures in the photo pages have that staying power. Each has been reprinted countless times. Each has been seen by millions of people around the globe, speaking in the universal language of photography. Somehow, perhaps because they are pictures of real people and events, each one has had the power to change the way people think and feel.

March, 1936—Migrant mother

The woman in this photo is a 32-year-old mother of seven. Camped beside a field, her family had just sold the tires off their car to buy food. The photo, taken during the Great Depression, still carries the unforgettable message, "What will happen to us now?"

In the 1930s, many people in the Canadian Prairies and American Midwest abandoned their failing farms. Rather than starve, they loaded their families and belongings into trucks and cars and set out for places like California to look for a better life. But the "migrant workers," as they were called, often found only more hunger and despair.

The young woman who took this photo, Dorothea Lange, became one of the most famous American photojournalists. Her remarkable pictures helped to focus attention on the plight of the homeless farm workers.

May 6, 1937—The *Hindenburg* explosion

The giant airship *Hindenburg* carried 97 passengers in luxurious comfort across the Atlantic from Germany to the U.S.A. As it was coming in for a landing, news photographers prepared to document the historic event. Unlike today's helium-filled blimps, the *Hindenburg* was filled with highly flammable hydrogen gas.

Suddenly, just before touching down, the *Hindenburg* burst into flames. Within minutes it had burned to ashes and 33 people were dead. Later, photos of the flaming airship flashed around the globe on newspapers, magazine covers, and movie screens. These startling images spelled the end of the airship as an important mode of transportation.

April 19, 1943—The Warsaw Ghetto uprising

No one knows who took the photo of the frightened little boy in the streets of Warsaw. We can imagine how he felt as he and his family were taken from their home and rounded up by Nazi soldiers.

In 1939, at the start of World War II, Nazi Germany invaded Poland. All Jewish people living in the capital, Warsaw, were ordered to resettle in a slum area, where they were allowed barely enough food and fuel to survive the long cold winters.

The young people began an armed resistance. The Germans responded by bombing and burning the ghetto where they lived. Over 56 000 people living there were captured or killed. Miraculously, the six-year-old boy in this photograph survived. After the war, this photo was found in the files of a Nazi commander and it was used as evidence in the trials of Nazi leaders for war crimes.

1946—Gandhi beside his spinning wheel

A quiet figure sits on the floor beside a spinning

wheel. The man was Mahatma Gandhi, loved and respected by millions of people. This photo by Margaret Bourke-White is probably the best-known portrait of the revered Indian leader.

Bourke-White had a tight deadline when she flew to India to photograph Gandhi for *LIFE* magazine. Gandhi was an important world figure. He was trying to win India's independence from Britain without violence, through a program of passive resistance.

Gandhi wouldn't allow Bourke-White to take his picture until she learned to use the Indian spinning wheel or *charka*. Perhaps he thought it would help her to understand him better. She struggled with the *charka* as her deadline pressed nearer. Finally she mastered it and snapped the photo just in time to meet *LIFE*'s deadline.

July 31, 1969—Earthrise

Bathed in sunlight, the beautiful blue planet rises into view above the lunar surface. This is what the astronauts saw through the window of *Apollo 11*, while orbiting the moon.

From this viewpoint, the world looks small, fragile, and incredibly beautiful. Spaceship Earth, as the environmental movement has called it, seems to deserve our care and protection.

Although interest in space exploration has

waned since the 1960s, this photo remains as one of the high points of the space programs of that period. It has fundamentally changed the way we view the earth.

November 12, 1989—Fall of the Berlin Wall

The wall is down. Photos show people celebrating by dancing on the wall, painting on the wall and chipping pieces off to carry away. There was no one to stop them. For the first time since the wall was built in 1961 there was no one to shout "Halt," no one to shoot if you didn't. The Berlin Wall became the scene of a giant party.

The image of the crumbling wall sent waves of hope and excitement around the world. The Berlin Wall had come to stand for the division between two sides in the cold war, between east and west.

All this ended in November, 1989. Without violence, the wall went down. East and West Germany were united and German youth trampled on the ruins of the wall that had divided them.

March, 1936—Migrant mother

("Unforgettable Photos," p. 44)

May 6, 1937—The
Hindenburg explosion
("Unforgettable
Photos," p. 44)

April 19, 1943—
The Warsaw
Ghetto uprising

("Unforgettable
Photos," p. 44)

1946—Gandhi
("Unforgettable
Photos," p. 44)

July 31, 1969—Earthrise
("Unforgettable Photos," p. 44)

November 12, 1989—Fall of the Berlin Wall

(*"Unforgettable Photos,"* p. 44)

Charlie Chaplin as the "Little Tramp"
(p. 18)

Juicy Fruit gum
transit ads
("Multicultural
Advertising,"
p. 56)

WHAT'S NEWS?

by Andrew A. Rooney

News reporting is supposed to be objective,
but there are usually two, or more, sides to
every story.

A young reporter I talked with last weekend
said he was in trouble with his readers and with
the police because of a story he'd written.

His newspaper is in a medium-sized city in
the Northeast [United States] and the incident
involved a holdup of a small grocery store. The two
men who did it were chased into a dead-end alley
and caught by three men who heard the grocer yell
for help as the thieves ran out of his store.

The two men were not armed and when they
were caught, they were pinned to the ground while
someone called the police.

The reporter heard of the chase over his police
radio and raced to the scene, arriving at about the

same time as the cops.

The two suspects were released by their captors and they stood up to face the police. One of them made a smartass remark in answer to one of the cop's questions and the cop instantly pistol-whipped him to the ground and went after him again with his feet.

At this point one of the three men who had originally captured the robber pulled the cop off and told him to cool it.

When the reporter got back to the office, he realized there were three ways to write the story. It could be the grocer's story of the robbery, it could be the story of the three citizens capturing the thieves or it could be the story of the cop beating one of the robbers.

The reporter wrote the story of the policeman beating the thief.

"You wrote the wrong story," a cop said to him after the story appeared. "Those two guys were guilty as hell."

The reporter has since been reprimanded by several cops he knows and by half a dozen letter-writing readers.

A lot of newspaper readers and almost all cops would agree that the story should have been about the holdup and the capture, not about police brutality. Not many newspaper editors would, though. They'd agree the emphasis should have been where this reporter put it: MAN BITES DOG.

It seems to me there's a news crisis in the world. The crisis has nothing to do with world events but with events in the news business itself. It has become such a big business that there is inevitable pressure for the product to make money.

This is a reasonable enough expectation for owners and stockholders but most newsmen and women like to think that news is more important than money. To increase profit on a product, you have to increase its popularity. Making news more popular is the last resort of a dying news operation.

If news is treated like any other product being sold for money, then it will be made the way people like it. Newspapers will print what people want to read, not what they ought to know. Reporters will ignore stories of police brutality because no one likes to read about it. "Those two had it coming to them."

In London during the Falkland Islands war [in 1982], Margaret Thatcher complained about a BBC news broadcast that suggested that the death of a husband was just as sad for a woman in Argentina as it was for the wife of a British sailor.

Margaret didn't like that.

"The case for our country is not being put with sufficient vigour by certain journalists," she said.

Mrs. Thatcher was answered by a spokesman for the BBC.

"It is not the BBC's role to boost troops' morale or to rally British people to the flag," he said. "What we are about is not propaganda but information."

Whether a journalist is reporting a war or a grocery store holdup, it is not his business to consider whether the story will do good or harm. He has to have faith that in the long run, the truth will do good. The policeman did beat the thief. It was unusual. *It* was the news story.

The reporter was my son, Brian, too.

▲▼▶▼▶▲▼▶▼▶▲▼▶▼▶▲▼▶▼▶▲▼▶▼▶▶

ON DRAWING THE LINE

by Christie Blatchford

How far should a news reporter go to get a
hot story? And where do you draw the line?
Canadian columnist Christie Blatchford
shares one of her experiences.

A long time ago, before we had heard of Jim
Keegstra or Ernst Zundel, I did a story about a man
named Don Andrews. I was still in school, at
Ryerson in Toronto, and wanted to do a so-called
investigative piece about Andrews, then the head
of a right-wing group called the Western Guard.
(This, incidentally, was before my uncle Tom, a
great newspaperman, took me aside and told me
that all reporting should, by definition, be investigative.) The Guard, though primarily anti-Jewish,
was also anti-black, anti-Pakistani, anti-
homosexual, and anti-just about everything and
everyone in the country.

They were listed in the phone book (there were two numbers, I think, one a taped "White Power" message, the other a simple answering machine), and I called and left a message saying I was interested in joining the group. A few days later I talked to Andrews on the phone and arranged a tour of the group's office, never mentioning that I was a reporter.

I don't remember where it was, only a little about what it was like—decorated with pictures of Hitler and other prominent Nazis, German flags everywhere, bits of the Guard's nasty pamphlets on the wall. There were several young Guard types there on my visit, scary, small-eyed men in their late teens and early twenties. I talked for a while to Andrews, listening to him describe how the Guard was "protecting" whites' rights against invasive minorities, and thought, by my nods and questions, that I had him convinced I was legitimate. He wasn't sold, though; he proposed that a week or so later I come back and hand out some Guard literature.

On the appointed day, I turned up. Andrews and I and several of the young men got into a van and drove out to the east end of the city; I remember, as we travelled, one of the young guys spotting some people in turbans and shouting out the window at them. It seemed to take forever, but finally we got where Andrews wanted to go. "Okay," he said, "I want you to drop pamphlets at every house on this street."

And they let me out, with a stack of vile literature in my hands. I pretended to set off, hoping the van would disappear, but it didn't, not for a while. It cruised up the road a little.

I wanted, rather desperately, to pass the test, be accepted, and get more involved in the group. I wanted, in short, a story; and I wanted to nail them, but good. I tried; I walked up a few driveways, through a few gates, and actually dropped some pamphlets at a few houses. But I was humiliated and I couldn't stop myself from reading what I was carrying—vicious stuff that called the Holocaust a "myth," that urged white Canadians to protest "easy" immigration laws. I lasted for those few houses, then ditched the pamphlets in a garbage can and ran like hell, away from Andrews, away from the young Guardsmen.

I ended up writing a story; it was published in the school paper. It wasn't half the story I could have got if I'd been able to stick it out and get Andrews to trust me, but I couldn't stomach any more. There are some lines, even for a great story, that you don't cross.

▲▼▼▶▲▼▶▼▲▼▶▼▶▲▼▶▼▲▶

MULTICULTURAL ADVERTISING

by Alison Cunliffe

It's taken a long time, but advertisers, finally, are reflecting the variety of people in our society.

The boys are, as fashion-conscious teens often do, wearing their baseball caps backward.

Two of the faces under the caps are Caucasian. One is Asian. One is black and he's sporting a piece of gum where the adjustable head-band of a baseball cap usually sits in mid-forehead.

"Taste that sticks out," says the slogan on the ad. It's one of three transit ads that Wrigley Canada Inc. says is its most successful campaign ever, and it's a sign of the changing face of advertising.

Part of the reason for the success, says Wrigley marketing manager Mary Griffith, is that the ad portrays how young city dwellers look and will increasingly look: white, brown, black. East meets West with stop-offs everywhere else around the world.

Almost half of Toronto's population is expected to be visible minorities by the year 2001, according to a Carleton University study. Across Canada it will be close to one in five.

As a result, there will be more ads that show Canadians in all their diversity, says Suzanne Keeler, vice-president of public and business affairs at the Canadian Advertising Foundation.

More diverse advertising not only makes sense but can also make money.

Within six months of their new ads, Juicy Fruit's brand share leapt almost a full percentage point, worth about $640 000 a year in sales, in what Griffith calls a phenomenal response. Compared with a year earlier, retail sales of the sugar-based gum suddenly started beating the competition by seven percent.

"There just wasn't anything else going on at the time, other than this ad campaign, to account for this kind of performance," Griffith says.

"The strength of the campaign wasn't only because it was showing visible minorities. It also appealed to teens in their style, fun with fashion. But showing the kids the way they really look was certainly a part of the appeal."

IT'S A *MAD*, *MAD* WORLD!

by Karen Lawrence

"What, me worry?" says Alfred E. Neuman, the freckled, gap-toothed mascot of *MAD* magazine. But a generation of parents all over North America *did* worry as their children eagerly read the magazine's pages. No wonder. *MAD* pokes fun at practically everything the adult world stands for.

There has never been another magazine like *MAD*.

First of all, *MAD* has no ads. In the 1950s *MAD*'s founder, William Gaines, realized that he could not make fun of advertising and advertisers and still sell ads for his magazine. It was one or the other. Gaines made the bold decision to rely on subscriptions and newsstand sales to keep the magazine afloat—and it worked. Readers, especially young readers, subscribed by the millions.

If *MAD* looks and feels like a comic book, it isn't surprising. William Gaines' father, Max, invented the comic book. Back in the 1930s, during the Great Depression, Max Gaines put together comic strips from the newspaper in book form. His company, EC Publications, became one of the great success stories of the decade.

When Max died in 1947, his son William took over his father's comic-book business at the age of 25. William Gaines stayed in school while running the business, graduating from New York University in 1948. He soon changed the company's name from Educational Comics to Entertaining Comics, but kept the EC label.

Gaines got the idea of a satiric comic book in the '50s, at a time when the United States was experiencing strong censorship, especially in the movies. Gaines thought that a comic book—not considered a serious art form by most people—would escape the attention of censors. The first issue of *MAD* appeared in 1952. It contained four stories, each making fun of an EC comic book such as *The Vault of Horror* and *The Crypt of Terror*.

Over the years, *MAD* has attacked anything and everything in society that takes itself too seriously, or pretends to be something it isn't. Spoofs of movies, TV shows, and advertisements are favourite features (see the "ads" at the end of this article). Parents have a tough time in the pages of *MAD*, as do politicians, big corporations, and other symbols of authority. *MAD* usually takes the young person's point of view, embodied in Alfred E. Neuman, the forever boyish, cheeky figure who appears on every cover. His motto, "What, me worry?" captures the casual, irreverent attitude of a particular age group.

Smart-aleck puns (some people would call them stupid) are a mainstay of *MAD*'s writing style. Here's a sample from the table of contents of a recent issue:

ONE FOOTNOTE IN THE GRAVE DEPARTMENT

WHEN IRISH SPIES ARE SMILING DEPARTMENT

MAD writers like Al Jaffee have become famous for such features as "Snappy Answers to Stupid Questions."

MAD's visual style is just as famous. The detailed caricatures are wickedly accurate—you can always recognize the famous figures being made fun of.

Hugely popular during the baby-boom years of the 1960s and '70s, *MAD* doesn't have as many readers as it used to, but it still has a devoted following. Comedians who grew up with *MAD* adapted its tone and style for TV shows like *Saturday*

Night Live. Other magazines, such as *National Lampoon, Spy*, and *Frank*, follow the trail blazed by *MAD*. It's hard to realize that, before *MAD*, there were few parodies of advertising and TV. Of course, along the way *MAD* has made some enemies. Many of its features are in terrible taste. But they are always well-drawn and funny, if a bit warped.

William Gaines died in 1992, and his death was mourned in the *New York Daily News* with an obituary titled "WHAT, ME DEAD?" In letters, readers talked about their feelings for Gaines and what *MAD* meant to them while growing up. They knew they would miss the man who taught them to laugh at everything—particularly the absurdity of advertising and the media.

NEW EXTRA STRENGTH

ANASPRIN

CONQUERS HEADACHES WITH 43% MORE PAIN RELIEVERS

Actually, this is just another way of saying that old, regular strength *Anasprin* failed to cure most headaches because it contained 43% less pain relievers! And that might explain why you and millions of others tried our product once, and then never bought it again! Now we're praying you'll be sufficiently impressed with this ad to give us another try, and discover whether *Anasprin* has improved enough to compete with other famous brands.

ANASPRIN

A PRODUCT OF MEGABUCK DRUGS, INC.
"Your Suffering Is Our Business"

THE GREATEST THING YOU'VE EVER EATEN!

BURGER BARN'S NEW
TURKEY-ON-TOASTY

Bet you think it's strange that we've suddenly stopped touting our yummy hamburgers, and started telling you that turkey sandwiches are better! Well, we've got a reason! Even the gristly beef we serve has gotten so expensive that we now have to charge $2.25 for a hamburger to break even! But we can still get rich selling you ground turkey parts for $1.50! So join the suckers eating our latest fast-food gimmick—Turkey-On-Toasty!

BURGER BARN

LOOK FOR OUR OLD FAMILIAR SIGN (WHICH WE'LL CHANGE IF THIS NEW GIMMICK EVER CATCHES ON)!

HOME OF THE TURKEY ON TOASTY

We've been selling paper towels for 58 years, so it's somewhat embarrassing to admit we needed all that time to perfect our product! Hopefully, you'll be so grateful Scoff Towels Don't fall apart quite as badly when wet as they used to that you won't even think about the hardships your mother suffered just because it took us so long to come up with a trivial thing like adding one extra ply! We're truly sorry, and we beg you to forgive us for three generations of peddling defective trash!

NEW DOUBLE-STRENGTH SCOFF TOWELS

"So Simple We Should've Thought Of It Half A Century Ago!"

3

On the Air:
Television and Radio

▲ ▽ ▷ ▽ ▲ ▽ ▷ ▲ ▷ ▽ ▲ ▷ ▽ ▲ ▷ ▽ ▲ ▽ ▷ ▷

THE FAR SIDE
by Gary Larson

Why we see news anchorpersons only
from the waist up.

▲ ▽ ▷ ▽ ▲ ▽ ▷ ▽ ▲ ▽ ▷ ▽ ▲ ▷ ▽ ▲ ▷ ▽ ▷

TELEVISION AND RADIO TRIVIA

Collected by Todd Mercer

Television Trivia

Amount of time teenagers watch television on an average day: 3 hours

Amount of time adults watch television on an average day: 3 hours, 20 minutes

Most cars wrecked over the course of a television series (*Dukes of Hazzard*): 300

Percentage of teens who flip the channel even when their favourite show is on: 74%

Percentage of teens who agree that commercials are a fair price to pay for free television: 73%

Number of Canadians who watch the *MuchMusic* channel at any given moment: 200 000

Percentage of respondents to a *TV Guide* survey who said they wouldn't give up watching television for $1 million: 25%

Number of participants in the All-Japan High School Quiz Championships: 80 799

Number of times a day that the original *Star Trek* TV series is broadcast throughout the United States: 200

Radio Trivia

Average amount of time per week that teens listen to radio: 13.4 hours

Highest number of calls recorded to a radio talk show: 388 299

Number of seconds by which tuning a radio while driving reduces a driver's reaction time: 0.7

Top prize won by a teen on a radio quiz show: $1 000 000

Percentage of vinyl, tape, and compact-disc sales in Canada accounted for by rock or rock-oriented music: 66%

Price paid for one of singer Michael Jackson's white gloves: $35 475

Estimated cost of record contracts signed in 1991 by Sony Music Entertainment Inc. and Virgin Records with singers Michael and Janet Jackson: $119.4 million

GETTING THE NEWS

Interviews edited by Linda Frum

Canada's top TV journalists give us the scoop on the sometimes dangerous, sometimes emotional—but always exciting—job of bringing us the evening news.

Eve Savory

Whatever a reporter's views on the right to privacy of public figures, CBC science and medical reporter Eve Savory tries to protect the dignity of her less well-known subjects, even as she exposes their suffering.

For a piece on euthanasia, I interviewed a woman who had Lou Gehrig's disease, which paralyzes your entire body. All she could move was her eyes. She was weeks from death. I asked her if she wanted the doctors to take "heroic measures" to end her life. Because she couldn't speak, all she could do was move her eyes back and forth to signal that, "yes," she did. I went away and I just felt like I wanted to throw up.

Her husband sat next to her, weeping. He was feeding her chocolates. She wasn't allowed to have them and they would melt on her lips. She couldn't swallow, and chocolate trickled down her neck. It was heartbreaking. As we filmed this, I had this sense of terrible invasion into someone's dying moments.

I found the physician who was in charge of palliative care[1], and I told her I was really traumatized by the interview. I didn't know if I should put it on the air. The doctor said, "You should know that Mrs. MacDonald wanted so much to do this. It was her way of leaving the world something and feeling like her death was not totally in vain."

It touched me so much that this woman wanted to leave something positive behind. Sure, I invade people's space at times. But I never do it without making it really clear what type of invasion it is going to be. I always talk with the camera operator to make sure these stories are done as sensitively as possible. The story of Mrs. MacDonald really mattered.

Once I understood that people let you into their lives for a reason, I felt better about what I do. What's more, if I can tell their story in such a way that they do not feel betrayed or raped, then I feel I've done something good.

Malcolm Fox

CTV field producer Malcolm Fox is reluctant to shelter his audience from grisly scenes. He places realism—even graphic realism—ahead of squeamish sensibilities.

We spent a week at the site of the Italian earthquake in 1976 so we could follow the process of digging through the rubble and finding victims. Of the scenes we saw there, the one I remember the most vividly is of an unearthed father, dressed in his underwear, lying on a couch with his year-old daughter in his arms. Their house had fallen down on top of them. We rolled film while people were uncovering them.

In those days, the decision of what the audience would see was made in Toronto and not in the field. We would send back the film, the script, the on-camera portions, and it would be assembled in Toronto. Today, the decision of what to show is made in the field. I always err on the liberal side. I believe we should be a window on the world. If it happened, we should show it. If the story is, this father tried to save his daughter and the house fell down on top of them, well then, however gory these pictures may be, they should be shown. It is possible to cut the pictures in such a way that they illustrate without dwelling on the gore.

1. **palliative care**: palliative care relieves pain, but does not cure the ailment

▲▼▶▼▶▲▼▶▼▶▲▼▶▼▶▲▼▶▼▶

OPRAH—ON RADIO

by Robert Waldron

Oprah Winfrey is host of her own syndicated
TV talk show and the highest-paid woman in
show business. But she actually got her start
in the early 1970s, at age 17, as a radio news-
caster in her home town of Nashville,
Tennessee.

While looking for people to sponsor her in the
March of Dimes walkathon, Oprah wandered into
the studios of Nashville radio station WVOL,
which were near her home. Since it was early afternoon and most of the station's employees were out
to lunch, Oprah had difficulty finding someone at
the station willing to put up money for her walk.
Just as Oprah was about to leave the station, John
Heidelberg, WVOL's friendly disk jockey, was
returning from lunch. A station employee quickly
asked Oprah to wait a minute. Introducing John to

Oprah, she said, "Maybe he can help you."

With a winning smile and a confident manner, Oprah explained to John why she was at the station. "I asked her what the walkathon was all about," John recalls. "She explained that she walked so many miles and I would have to pay for the number of miles she walked. That was pretty much all there was to it. I told her, 'Sure, I'll do it.' " Successful at finding another sponsor, Oprah left the station beaming. Meanwhile, John went on the air and immediately put the incident out of his head.

A few weeks later Oprah returned to WVOL and told John, "Well, I'm here to collect the money." Suddenly remembering that he had, in fact, pledged to support her walk, John willingly paid her. Oprah's second encounter with John left an impression.

"I admired her voice," he says. "She was very articulate. Her grammar was very good." This struck a chord with John, who prided himself on being articulate and using good grammar whenever possible. "I'm from outside the boondocks of Mississippi," he continues. "The concept and image that people get of blacks living in the South can sometimes be very negative. I watched an old Western when I was a young man and was very impressed by a gentleman in it who could speak very well. I said, 'Someday I'll do that.' I just liked hearing that in people. And Oprah had it. I thought, 'Hey, here's a young lady who can go places.'"

John asked Oprah if she had ever considered a career in broadcasting. "She hadn't given it any thought at all. But the voice was there."

John told Oprah about the qualities he felt she possessed and asked if she would be interested in possibly working in radio. He then asked Oprah if she would be willing to make a tape for him. Oprah responded, "Sure."

"I took her into the newsroom. I ripped some copy off the news wire and asked her to read it. I told her that way I'd have something to show the station manager so he could hear what she sounded like."

Stepping up to a mike, Oprah read the copy. Listening to her, John observed that, besides having a rich, deep, clear voice, Oprah had another quality that was vital for anyone who wanted to succeed in radio. "Radio's a companion," he explains. "People out there listening want that person on the radio to be warm, affectionate. They want that person to talk to them, not at them. The listener wants to relate. He wants to be able to say, 'Hey, that's my friend. I know him.' He can call him up and say, 'Hey, Buddy, this is so and so.' The guy knows

Buddy. He may not have seen him, but he knows him like he's his friend." John saw in Oprah her potential for being the listener's friend. "She had a very warm personality." Taking Oprah's tape, John promised to let WVOL's station manager, Noble Blackwell, listen to it and said he would get back to her. John imagined Oprah doing newscasts.

At that time, however, during the early seventies, women, for the most part, were still relegated to offering female listeners recipes and household hints. "It was hard for women to get into radio," John recalls. When the Federal Communications Commission required radio stations to begin affirmative action programs, things began to change. "Station managers hired them because they needed a minority. They felt like, 'Well, we've gotta protect our licence, so we'll hire some females.' "

John played Oprah's demo tape for Noble Blackwell and he said, "That does sound pretty good." When he played the demo for other people in management at WVOL, however, they were less optimistic about Oprah's potential. After all, they reasoned, she's only a 17-year-old kid. "But I convinced them that here was a young lady who had a lot of the things we were looking for and to give her a break," says John. "Eventually, we did give her a break."

Oprah was hired to work part-time on the

weekends doing news. "John really did discover Oprah," says Dana Davidson, who, like Oprah, got her start at WVOL, and has been with the station since the late sixties.

"I feel like I was a catalyst. I'm sure she would've made it at one point or another. You just don't hold that kind of talent back," acknowledges John. "I feel good knowing I had a hand in shaping some things."

"You don't just go into radio and start performing. You go through a training period," explains Dana, discussing WVOL's policy for hiring undeveloped talent. For the first few weekends Oprah worked at WVOL she didn't receive a salary. John kept her busy teaching her the basics. "At that time there was nothing outstanding that would make you think there was anything out of the ordinary. She was an average employee."

"Ope knew that she had something on the ball," says John. "She didn't feel intimidated or threatened by anything. That was one of the things that caught my eye. It was like she wasn't worried about anything. Nothing bothered her."

"She was aggressive," adds Dana. "Not at all shy. She knew where she was going."

After a few short weeks at WVOL, Oprah was receiving a weekly salary of a hundred dollars. In addition to performing newscasts at the station on the weekends, Oprah started coming in for a few hours weekdays after school. She joked to a reporter that one of the reasons she accepted the job at WVOL was because, without "Leave It to Beaver" to watch in the afternoon, it gave her something to do.

by Jeff MacNelly

HI & LOIS

written by Brian and Greg Walker;
art by Chance Browne

▲ ▶ ▶ ▼ ▶ ▲ ▼ ▶ ▼ ▶ ▲ ▼ ▶ ▼ ▶ ▲ ▼ ▶ ▼ ▶ ▶

PUNCH MUCH OR PUNCH OUT MUCH: ROCK VIDEOS

by Jeff Bateman

Do rock videos actually help to sell music albums, or are they an expensive—but unnecessary—gimmick?

The skeptics said it would never fly. Rock'n'roll, they argued, was engineered for nightclubs, concert halls, and home and car stereos. On TV it had mostly been a bust. The only show to survive for more than a season or two was Dick Clark's legendary *American Bandstand*.

The skeptics were wrong. Music television— MTV in the United States, MuchMusic, *Video Hits*, MusiquePlus, *Rock'n'Talk*, *Good Rockin' Tonite* in Canada—has proved the small screen can shake, rattle, and roll round-the-clock. In fact, since MTV's arrival in 1981 video has forever changed the way we consume music.

Radio, traditionally the source of the hottest of hits, has lost its place as taste-maker and trend-setter. Nowadays we punch Much to mainline the newest, sharpest, and flashiest in sights and sounds. We stay up past midnight watching *Good Rockin' Tonite* because it's guaranteed top-30 fresh. The same can't be said for most radio stations, which mainly play classic-rock oldies that passed their sell-by date years ago.

"The music business still regards radio as our number-one tool for breaking records," says Ken Ashdown of PolyGram Records of Canada, "but video is a very close second. This is a visual age, and it's very hard to sell a product of any kind without visuals. Videos give music that extra dimension."

Think only of the hype surrounding the premiere of Michael Jackson's *Black or White*. The song was nothing special, but the video was pure marketing genius. Its face-melding sequence set new standards in film trickery.

It's no surprise MTV and MuchMusic (launched in September 1984) have survived and prospered. Popular music has always reached bigger audiences when it takes the time to marry sound with vision.

In Hollywood's golden age, the movie musical was hugely popular and as a result, stars like

Fred Astaire and Judy Garland enjoyed successful recording careers. Rock'n'roll got an early boost in such flicks as *The Girl Can't Help It* (featuring Little Richard), while Elvis Presley's fame rocketed with his infamous appearance on *The Ed Sullivan Show* (censors were so alarmed by his provocative hip-shake that they insisted he be filmed from the waist up). The Beatles, fed up with screamathon concerts, made the film *A Magical Mystery Tour* (1967) to satisfy their fans and their own artistic ambitions.

By the mid-eighties, the music business had discovered an important fact: a $30 000 video could introduce an unknown group to a million viewers and create instant stars based on one hot song and one memorable clip.

"That was a tremendously exciting time," recalls MuchMusic VJ Kim Clarke Champniss. "Me and my friends would gather around the TV and check out great bands from Britain like Depeche Mode and Duran Duran. The music was one thing, but there were also the haircuts, the look, the stance—videos let us know what was cool and what wasn't."

The average video viewer is what MuchMusic terms a "grazer." He or she roams restlessly across the cable-TV spectrum, channel-zapper working overtime. When viewers do stop at video channels like MTV, they generally stick around for no more than 15 minutes at a time.

What holds our interest are either the biggest of stars or the best in video art. Some artists treat video as a serious and fun means of creative expression. Yet there are many more die-hards who think differently. Mark Knopfler, leader of Dire Straits, refuses to appear in clips promoting his songs. "It's not my business to go around telling everybody what the song is about, which is why I don't like videos," he explains. "I feel videos spoil a song; they shut it down, almost like a poor film of a good book."

Knopfler is among those who believe video is killing rock'n'roll through slick Hollywoodization. Other critics say that if not for music television we'd have been spared the lip-synching fraud of Milli Vanilli. Then there's the sexism that runs through certain videos, most notably the Robert Palmer clip (*Addicted to Love*) that featured a bevy of identical, mini-skirted models. Many videos are plain stupid.

Guilty on all counts, admit those involved in the video industry, but what else is new? This is rock'n'roll, after all, the last frontier of all that is cheap, silly, fun, and fleeting. Besides, when a band with great videos comes along, the criticisms are irrelevant.

Video has certainly added to the debt load

carried by recording artists. The production of a clip usually requires the same extensive crew of filmmakers and stagehands associated with any TV production. The union-scale rates add up fast, and there's absolutely no guarantee that the video will win regular airplay.

Sale of music-video collections can recover some of this investment, but usually only for those groups with diehard fans who want every last product associated with their heroes. "Kiss, Metallica—their videos move almost as fast as *Terminator II*," says Sam the Record Man's Richard Hobbs. "We also get steady sales on Hall-of-Fame artists like Rod Stewart, Bob Dylan, and The Doors."

Times are changing, though. A growing number of record stores like Sam's and HMV Canada carry videos because TV monitors and VCRs have been integrated into home entertainment systems. Why just buy a CD or tape, when you get the same music and sound quality plus pictures to match? "That's the way of the future," argues Hobbs.

This isn't great news for groups struggling to get their music heard. Perhaps they can scratch together enough to cover a studio bill, but a video shoot as well? Unsigned groups shouldn't worry about it, say the record companies; they still sign artists based on music and songs, not visuals.

Still, a video can help an unsigned group get coverage on local television or, in the rare case, MuchMusic. By being truly creative and utilizing the talents of film students who'll work for costs, a video bill can be kept to under $5000.

When all is said and done, video remains an accessory for music and artist. Just ask Boy George or Cyndi Lauper: the one-time king and queen of the video clip were crucified by their own images. Their records, good as some were, were too heavily disguised by pancake make-up and zany outfits to be taken seriously.

"Video is just one part of the package," concludes PolyGram's Ken Ashdown. "In the long run it's good people who are going to continue to outsell the rest. That's got nothing to do with visual gimmickry; it's due to great music and great talent."

STAR TREK QUIZ

by Michael Uslan and Bruce Solomon

Star Trek, in all its generations, is probably the most popular show ever to run on TV. Gene Roddenberry's vision of an intergalatic federation, where all races were respected, has captured the imagination of millions. If you're a "trekker," this quiz will be easy—if not, the answers follow.

Each question answered correctly about *Star Trek* is worth one point.

1. How many years was the mission of the starship for?

2. The name of the starship was _____.

3. Mr. Spock was filled with the green blood of a _____.

4. What was the name of the captain of the ship before Captain Kirk took command?

5. Which of the following crew members is not usually found on the bridge?
   a. Scotty   b. Mr. Sulu   c. Chekov   d. Uhura
   e. Spock

6. What was the name of the nurse on board?

7. What was Bones's real name?

8. What kind of cuddly alien life multiplies at a super-fast rate?

9. Who played Bones?

10. Jane Wyatt played the mother of Bud, Betty, and Kathy on *Father Knows Best*, but whose mother was she on *Star Trek*?

Answers

1. Five
2. The U.S.S. *Enterprise*
3. Vulcan
4. Captain Pike
5. a. Scotty
6. Christine Chapel
7. Dr. Leonard McCoy
8. Tribbles
9. DeForrest Kelly
10. Mr. Spock's

▲ ▶ ▶ ▽ ▲ ▼ ▶ ▶ ▽ ▲ ▼ ▶ ▶ ▽ ▲ ▼ ▶ ▼ ▶ ▶

INVADERS FROM MARS

by Carla Magor

"I can see the thing's body now—it's as large as a bear. It glistens like wet leather. But that face, it's … it's … ladies and gentlemen, it's indescribable!"

It was Hallowe'en night, 1938. Just as people today relax for the evening in front of their TV sets and VCRs, millions of people all over the United States were relaxing in front of their radios.

Most listeners were enjoying *Edgar Bergen's Comedy Hour*. Edgar Bergen (father of actress Candice Bergen) was a ventriloquist, who always made people laugh. Then Bergen introduced an unpopular singer, and people got up to turn the dial. In 1938, there were no remote controls, but changing stations was just as popular as it is today.

Suddenly, people heard the sobbing, terror-stricken voice of a radio announcer. The news was from New Jersey, and it was chilling. Reporting live from the scene, the announcer said that a cylinder of unknown origin had just slammed into the earth "with earthquake force" near Grover's Mill, New Jersey.

Listeners in millions of living rooms froze in their seats as the announcer's voice shook.

Ladies and gentlemen, this is the most terrifying thing I have ever witnessed—wait a minute! Someone's crawling out of the hollow top—someone or ... something. I can see peering out of that black hole two luminous discs. Maybe eyes, might be a face... Good heavens, something wriggling out of the shadow like a grey snake. Now it's another one... They look like tentacles... I can see the thing's body now—it's as large as a bear. It glistens like wet leather. But that face, it's ... it's ... ladies and gentlemen, it's indescribable; I can hardly force myself to keep looking at it, it's so awful. The eyes are black and gleam like a serpent; the mouth is ... kind of V-shaped, with saliva dripping from its rimless lips that seem to quiver and pulsate. The monster or whatever it is can hardly move; it seems weighted down possibly by gravity or something...

There was more. Much more. The monster turned its deadly heat ray on advancing soldiers and turned them into screaming pillars of fire. The fire was spreading—then, abruptly, the announcer's voice was cut off. There was a brief musical break, and then bulletins started to pour in:

"Red Cross emergency workers dispatched to the scene…"

"Bridges hopelessly clogged with human traffic…"

"The strange beings who landed in the Jersey farmland tonight are the vanguard of an invading army from the planet Mars…"

"The monster is now in control of the middle section of New Jersey…"

Air-force bombers, the report continued, were melting out of the sky. New York City itself was now under attack. Smoke and poisonous gas filled the night air, drifting across the city.

By this time, people listening to the radio had leapt to their feet and were calling the police and running through the streets. Like wildfire, the word spread to those who weren't listening to the radio—the United States was being invaded by Martians!

Inside Studio One at CBS in New York, Orson Welles and his fellow actors kept on broadcasting. They had no idea of what was happening outside their door, in the city's streets, and across the country. They continued with their radio adaptation of *The War of the Worlds*, H. G. Wells's science-fiction novel. Little did they realize that most of their listeners had missed the opening of *Mercury Theater on the Air*, when Orson Welles explained that the program was a dramatization.

Toward the end of the radio play, Welles, playing a professor named Pierson, described the scene. He was in Times Square, he said, staggering through the destruction caused by the Martian heat rays. The city was deserted. He pressed on to Central Park. There he found the remains of the Martians themselves. They were dead—victims of Earth germs! The Martians, said Professor Pierson, had no immunity to earth diseases and had all been destroyed. Earth was now safe.

Even before the end of the broadcast, Welles and the other actors had begun to realize that something was wrong. At one point, CBS had interrupted the broadcast to announce that it was just a play. Welles closed the show by calling it "Mercury Theater's own radio version of dressing up in a sheet and jumping out of a bush and saying boo" for Hallowe'en.

But it was too late. Police, wielding clubs, stormed through the halls of CBS. Outside the studio a huge swarm of reporters and police were waiting for Welles. Reports were coming in from other media that panic-stricken listeners, convinced that the broadcast was real, not fiction, had died or committed suicide.

Welles went to face the crowd, certain that his acting career was finished. But, although millions were badly frightened that Hallowe'en night, miraculously, no one died or was even badly injured. And, as a result of the publicity, Orson Welles was an overnight sensation. He went on to become one of Hollywood's most celebrated directors and actors, and *The War of the Worlds* became the most famous radio show ever broadcast.

ACKNOWLEDGEMENTS

Permission to reprint copyright material is gratefully acknowledged. Every reasonable effort to trace the copyright holders of materials appearing in this book has been made. Information that will enable the publisher to rectify any error or omission will be welcomed.

Mother Goose and Grimm by Mike Peters, © 1993 Grimmy Inc. Used with permission of Tribune Media Services.

Special-Effects Dinosaurs Look Like the Real Thing by Craig MacInnis reprinted with permission – The Toronto Star Syndicate. Excerpted from "Dinosaur actors look real and listen to the director," published in *The Toronto Star*, July 11, 1993.

The Golden Age of Laughter by Max Braithwaite from *Never Sleep Three In a Bed* by Max Braithwaite. Used [in Canada] by permission of the Canadian Publishers, McClelland & Stewart, Toronto. Reprinted [in U.S.A.] by permission of Curtis Brown, Ltd. Copyright © 1969 by Max Braithwaite.

Charlie Chaplin, the Little Tramp by Lorraine Monk from *Photographs That Changed the World* by Lorraine Monk, published in Canada by Macfarlane Walter & Ross and in the United States by Doubleday Inc.

Three-Kleenex Movies by Peg Kehret from *Winning Monologs for Young Actors* by Peg Kehret © 1986 Meriwether Publishing Ltd., 885 Elkton Drive, Colorado Springs, CO 80907.

The People in Movies: The following adaptation is reprinted courtesy of *Sports Illustrated for Kids* from the February 1993 issue. Copyright © 1993, Time Inc. Original article is titled "Picture a movie where everyone plays a leading role" (author not listed). All Rights Reserved.

Behind the Scenes: Casting Agent and Set Builder from *TG Magazine*. Reprinted with permission by TG Magazine, 202 Cleveland St., Toronto, ON, M4S 2W6, 416–487–3204.

Into the Future with Movies by Deborah Hitzeroth and Sharon Heerboth excerpted from *Movies: The World on Film* by Deborah Hitzeroth and Sharon Heerboth, © 1991 by Lucent Books, Inc. Reprinted by permission of the publisher.

Shoe by Jeff MacNelly reprinted by permission: Tribune Media Services.

Annie Leibovitz Shoots to Success by Becky Siamon © 1993 by Nelson Canada, A Division of Thomson Canada Ltd.

Unforgettable Photos © 1993 by Nelson Canada, A Division of Thomson Canada Ltd.

What's News by Andrew A. Rooney reprinted with the permission of Atheneum Publishers, an imprint of Macmillan Publishing Company from *Pieces of My Mind* by Andrew A. Rooney. Copyright © 1982, 1983, 1984 by Essay Productions, Inc.

On Drawing the Line by Christie Blatchford reprinted with permission from *Spectator Sports* by Christie Blatchford, published by Key Porter Books Limited, Toronto, Ontario. Copyright © 1986 Key Porter Books Limited.

Multicultural Advertising by Alison Cunliffe reprinted with permission – The Toronto Star Syndicate. Excerpted from "Ads with visible minorities win praise and boost sales," published in *The Toronto Star*, July 1, 1993.

It's a *MAD MAD* World! by Karen Lawrence © 1993 by Nelson Canada, A Division of Thomson Canada Ltd. *Artwork*: "Honest Ads That Introduce 'New, Improved' Products" was written by Tom Koch, illustrated by Bob Clarke and is used with permission from *MAD* Magazine © 1985 by E.C. Publications, Inc.

The Far Side by Gary Larson copyright © 1991 FarWorks, Inc. Dist. by Universal Press Syndicate. Reprinted with permission. All rights reserved.

Movie, Newspaper, Magazine, Television, and Radio Trivia collected by Todd Mercer has been gathered and adapted from the following sources:

"teens who flip the channel" statistic from the *Pepsi Street Beat Teen Survey* conducted by Decima Research; "teens who agree that commercials" statistic from *The Media Study*, Environics Research Group Limited, Toronto; 1992 IMAX Press Kit; Audit Bureau of Circulations, 1991; *Canada Year Book 1991*; *The Canadian Green Consumer Guide*; *The Globe and Mail*; *The Guiness Book of Movie Facts and Feats, 1991*; *The Guiness Book of World Records, 1993*; *1993 Information Please Almanac*; *It's A Fact* (Associated Press); *Marketing*, Sept. 14, 1992; *Newspaper Audience Databank, 1991*, The Toronto Star; *"Reader's Digest: Did You Know?"*, Reader's Digest, 1990; *Scholastic Update, 1993*; *The Toronto Star*; *The Usborne Book of Countries of the World of Facts*.

Getting the News by Linda Frum reprinted with permission from *The Newsmakers* edited by Linda Frum, published by Key Porter Books Limited, Toronto, Ontario. Copyright © 1990 Linda Frum.

Oprah—on Radio from the book *Oprah!* by Robert Waldron. Copyright © 1987 by Robert Waldron and reprinted with permission from St. Martin's Press, Inc., New York, NY.

Shoe by Jeff MacNelly reprinted by permission: Tribune Media Services.

Hi & Lois written by Brian and Greg Walker; art by Chance Browne. Reprinted with special permission of King Features Syndicate.

Punch Much or Punch Out Much: Rock Videos by Jeff Bateman reprinted with permission by *TG Magazine*, 202 Cleveland St., Toronto, ON, M4S 2W6, 416–487–3204.

***Star Trek* Quiz** by Michael Uslan and Bruce Solomon from *The TV Trivia Quiz Book* by Michael Uslan & Bruce Solomon. Copyright © 1979 by Michael Uslan & Bruce Solomon. Reprinted by permission from Crown Publishers, Inc.

Invaders from Mars by Carla Magor © 1993 by Nelson Canada, A Division of Thomson Canada Ltd.

THE EDITORS

Sharon Siamon is the author of ten novels for young readers as well as reviews and plays. She has been involved in numerous educational publications and is a contributing editor for *Owl* magazine. A former teacher, now living in Brighton, Ontario, she enjoys working with students and teachers in writing workshops.

James Barry is Chairman of the English Department at Brebeuf College School, North York, Ontario. He is the editor of the poetry anthologies *Themes on the Journey*, *Departures*, *Side by Side*, and *Poetry Express*, as well as an annual student writing anthology, *Triple Bronze*. Besides teaching, his special interests are sports (especially hockey), music, and student writing.